Olney

TABLE OF CONTENTS

Contributor Bios   52

Photography Contributor Bios   57

There is no sound like when the field of ten horses comes by the first time in front of the stands, and the moving gate pulls away and the horses fly toward the first turn, the iron shoes drumming the track, the silks, the leather, the motion.

-Maj Ragain

Olney Magazine
Fall 2021
Issue 2

Then, Changes

An Introduction

The thing about doing something like this, is that it takes work. In fact, it ends up being more work than you originally anticipated. Then, changes happen around you, in the world around you. When Tony and I started Olney Magazine, it seemed simple enough. We just wanted to make *something*. The reality is that once you make something, then it exists, and people know about it. Then they have opinions about it. Sometimes they're good and sometimes they're not. You don't get to control what happens next.

I've lost a lot of sleep this summer. It wasn't all just to keep the magazine going, but, sure, it definitely was a lot of it. Hell, this issue is already late, and I'm sitting here trying my damndest to write this introduction to it so that I can send the document away to our printers. If you're reading this, I can imagine that your summer was maybe filled with your own sleepless nights.

We all came into the season thinking a corner might be turned in the world, and then it didn't really happen. Shit is still bad. Somehow in the midst of it all, people are still writing poetry. Still reaching out into the echoless void. Still scratching out some bread for one another. I don't know how this will find you, paddling across the river of the world, but I do hope that it will find you.

When Tony wrote the introduction for the first issue, I was so impressed by his effortless way of connecting real feeling into his words. Whenever I read Tony's work it always has something behind it that comes across like an actual person wrote it. Being his friend for several years, I know how much he pours over every line break and word choice, but when I see it there on the page, it doesn't seem like it. This paragraph is in direct response to the nice things he had to say about me in Issue 1, in case you were wondering. But I do mean what I said.

I keep trying to land on something inspirational, something poignant to say to you, that will hit you square in your chest. The kind of phrase or notion that might make you pause and reflect before diving into the awesome work that people sent us for this issue, but nothing comes when I reach into the "cloud of unknowing", for thunder. I am hungry for changes. Eager to see them in myself and in the work we are doing. Excited at the prospect of the new. Hopeful that if you find yourself meandering through these pages, that it will be enough to get you through until the next one. From glory-to-glory, as they say.

Maybe someday I will meet you at the end of one of them, and you can tell me about it.

Brandon Noel
Co-editor & Founder

Laments, Supposedly

Ben Kline

I told the internet I was exhausted
of poems

then remembered Mom
telling a cousin I wasn't
a queer,

just *a witch*. Neither
were true

then. I was definitionless.
I chewed

and spit epithets, oats, knuckles,
foreskins. Once I

sugar tanked a bully's RV.

Maybe my fatigue
was the fight,

my fists gravel in his eye

when he caught me. Maybe
I flew
to fight more,

a crow with cataracts
perched in the alleys, silences

at dinner parties and on TV,
salt circles I drew

in the dark, my lighter
for old curtains.

Always old curtains

in the living rooms of the men who asked
no names. The drag queen who lived

above me during the W years
claimed those men

hated their mothers. I insisted
they loved them

too much. The curtains
were comfort. The beige

and olive damask a familiar touch,
a bully

chasing a youth their mothers
told them to leave.

Maybe I was a witch

because I saw what they held
in dark circles under their eyes

puffy, pink with unshed salts.
Mom claimed

I lied so well
I should write novels

about thieves or politicians,
not poems

lamenting plagues, corporeal
phantoms, statements she made
supposedly,

but she didn't
know poems

are colorful buttons, earrings
and bracelets left on the sill

by the murder.

MOTHER'S DAY, 2020

JEN GUPTA

His mother calls me Zen.
My mother still can't pronounce
his name. They are on opposite
sides of the world today, but
they both miss their children.
When he told her I existed, she tried
not to cry. When he told her
about the marriage, she knew
he was never coming home.

I don't know how to cook
fish stew. I always forget
to step away when he adds
the bay leaves to the sizzling oil.
Once, she called while
he was cooking and I was
taking a nap. We have

very few words in common.
When I say, it was nice talking
to you, she says, sure, sure
and it sounds like sarcasm
but she doesn't mean it that way,
I hope. My mother watches
me try on the wedding dress I ordered
online. He can't even send his
a card. This virus has built
a shield around his country
so we have no choice but
to make him part of mine.

I will wear a ring but not
vermillion powder in my part.
I am not her first choice but
I will keep trying. One day,
she will meet her daughter
-in-law for the first time.

I still won't know how to cook
fish stew but I will try
to add a few more words.
Namaste, mummyji. Soon,
we will stand in the backyard
where my mother taught me
how to plant a garden,
while his watches from
a screen, in the middle of
her night, as her only son
gives their name to me.

PROBABLY NEVER SEE YOU AGAIN IN THIS LIFE

SHANNON FROST GREENSTEIN

—after The Mountain Goats

Jenny calls from Montana / she's only passing through
Probably never see her again in this life I guess / not sure what I'm gonna do

How many times is it the last time;
an unintentional farewell, a symbiotic swan song,
before there will never again be a stage to share?

How many times do we fail to realize
we impact as we are impacted,
Truth in Phenomenology and Escher's doodling hands;
the butterfly effect holding sway over all.
Do we ever know we've missed the last chance
to say what hasn't been said?

How many times does that light go out,
the flame of human intimacy extinguished,
for every communal experience that can never be relived
because the last time together has come and gone
without anyone being aware?

Matthew, the alcoholic ex-boyfriend who was my first experience with love;
Jacqueline, the childhood best friend who inhabits my earliest memories;
Amanda, the frenemy against whom I once measured every facet of my being;
Lawrence, the first older man on whom I developed an agonizing crush;
Generic Frat Boy, who plied me with beer and took my virginity;
Kate, the roommate who lives in Europe, because who honestly wants to return to the USA *now*?
Daniel, who came out as Queer to me for the first time while I was studying in Australia;

How many times would we give anything to know
when it is the end, before it is the end;
when that cousin or neighbor or star-crossed lover
will no longer be in our lives
for the entirety of the rest of our lives?

How many times would we know what to say?
I'll probably never see you again in this life
"So please know…I love you."

Except for Generic Frat Boy. I would kick him in the balls instead.

I Press Shuffle & Taylor Swift Comes On

Sodiq Oyekanmi

while i bathe in cliff-side pools with my calamitous love

& insurmountable grief,

i remember the taste of R's love — saltwater mixed with blood.

picture a lover boy tangled with iron chains; mouth stuffed

with decayed flowers   & pain d r i p p i n g from his eyes.

nothing hurts more than misfired cupid arrows.   nothing hurts

more than falling — head first — into love

[without a helmet].   & this pool is but the mouth of hades

carpeted with asphodel   & dark faces

of boys like me who find a way to wash their souls   away

from their stained bodies.   & if somehow this pool refuses my body,

i hope this poem washes me

d

o

w

n

to the lakes where all the poet go to die.

Spring Date

Kevin Bertolero

Can you believe that morning we
woke early to eat little clementines
on the deck and watch the sun
creep through the white ash behind
Smith Chapel? It's okay to be
indulgent sometimes, I think,
to spend an extra few dollars at
Northwood Books, drink that
lavender lemonade they advertise
at Lil's Bakery where we go to get
a dozen crullers just for the two
of us to eat in the car on our
way to Portland. We take
Shore Road to see the rough surf
waves, stop for gas in what used
to be a little shipping town, now
just antique boats in the harbor
for the Bushes and out-of-state
tourists. You want to stop at the outlets
and we're sick from the donuts
so we walk by all the windows without
really going in to browse and then we
get to the gallery and you want to go in
and Dianne at the desk is so nice to us
because we're gay, and I think
this could be a nice future, you know,
being New England art gays
and you're wearing that little blue jacket
that makes your arms look sexy and
you give me a look like you
know exactly what I'm thinking.
Dianne makes a joke and we laugh
—not because she's funny, but because
she isn't.

Down the stairs there's the body of a horse. It releases a red ribbon. On the lawn we stomp cicadas, eat beetles. The head of the horse we storm to the roof. With it we mix an hourglass and a dash of lavender into a vinegar broth. To take a picture is to paint a paper. Only later will we cry. The hooves are scattered. We gather them like kids.

TRADITION

BENJAMIN NIESPODZIANY

—after Johannes Goransson

GOD'S BOY: RONNIE

ANDREW HAHN

the gospel of nicodemus says judas
told his wife goodbye before hanging himself
at the edge of the field of blood

the last time i saw ronnie i sashayed
in his six-inch steve madden stilettos
we performed choreography to pop music

we kissed in his bed   a slow unspooling
of our bodies   his black chest hair
caught between my teeth

judas wasn't an evil man   i don't think
he would have sold the savior for silver if God
didn't make him do it

ronnie publicly denounced his friends
to keep his salvation   i had tasted the snakeskin
on his tongue & felt it scrape the stubble on my neck

how could he have forgotten the game
of truth or dare   the naked night in the grass
laughing   trying to cover up what had been seen

the night after i slept in his bed
i attended the operetta in which he lay
flowers at a grave in candlelight

it was the most beautiful rendition of goodbye
the way he kissed me that night
tight-lipped & passionate   the light

kept from the room by paper blinds   like he knew
his current life was ending   like he knew
a field waited for him

MELANIE BROWNE

A LINE YOU JUST DON'T CROSS

Hubby is in hot water
He said he did not consider
himself a True Texan
the other day at Easter
and now he is sleeping
on the couch

I am making him do penance
by watching "Dallas" reruns
& he has to sing
yellow rose of Texas
while loading the dishwasher

Some people might think
I am going to extremes
but Ellie Ewing would
have done the same
thing while pouring
coffee from
a silver coffee-pot
on her 200 acre ranch

She throws parties
where everyone gets
drunk and then they
decide to ride horses
which seems like
a particularly bad idea

Portrait Titled After My Grandfather's Service

Okoli Stephen Nonso

—after reading Dalia Elhassan

when i talk about home, i talk about a body at rest,
or let's say home is the faces on the hilly landscape that hung on our wall.
in my grandfather's album are faces i no longer recognized.
the faces of my parents growing together,   a flip to the next,
just maami growing old   by herself.
memories of my dad are the vague — the foggy memories of a small child.

perhaps i should've told you first that my grandfather outlived his male children,
before death ate his remains.   you know,   when death wants to eat a
 body, she makes it vulnerable, then waits patiently, like vultures waiting
for a dying [insert animal] to become a carcass.
& yes, my grandfather fed his fears till it grew deep like
our ancestral river, eziudo to keep his body at rest.

you see, a year before my grandfather returned his flesh to earth, i wore his coat,
the lining was torn. he looked at me, then asked — how do you carry a body of
water without drowning? i rolled my eyes, i'd heard it before,
son dies. son dies. son dies. maybe death is a safe home for asylums.
or perhaps, death walks into a home, & eats where there's plenty of foods.

today, my grandfather goes home= a synonym for peace. & as I read his biography,
i circle familiar names in my mind /agufushi/   /ozoemenam/   /sunday/
who are living on the portrait that hung on our wall. i knew the Igbo
letters & its sounds, but could not spit out these names. I just read the end
with a period, because when grandfather passed, everything ended.
the pains in his body are buried with these names.

& now, i paint my grandfather's portrait, so it won't die again.

BEGINNING OF THE LUNAR YEAR

DALE COTTINGHAM

At one point I thought I knew
but that was long ago. More recently
I've taken to reading *Dilbert* who looks out
from his thin but colorful frame
of an office that could be anywhere. He stays energized
and in the groove by keeping a list of what he's got to do:
taking private messages off his voice mail,
riding waves with co-workers.
That livens the whole affair
and maintains him in ways he thought impossible before.

Then she called. My evening's looking up.
There will be thunder in the reaches,
some humorous negotiations over wine,
alternatives will be presented, claims adjusted,
a new accounting will be made.
I'm enthralled by the prospect.
I can see it now: I make smoke signals,
look for responses, offer a prayer
as if this were the beginning of the lunar year.

MOLECULE

—after Bob Heman

BENJAMIN
NIESPODZIANY

When the hut was finished, the animals moved to the roof. The basement remained a banquet hall only the tallest could attend. The dining room was lively, occupied by dignitaries. There was a wedding in the cellar. A struggle with the pipes. The funeral was unusual in that it happened at dawn. Casually long with an absence of God. When the weather allowed, the crowd grew symptoms. They armed the cars. Started wars with crows. The stars were high above and the fireflies were closer. The shovel in the snow was a wall for the frog.

DARKNESS

YUU IKEDA

Gradually,
darkness piles up
on her left hand

Her right hand
always runs through
her faded notebook
to soak pages
in darkness

Pages are filled with vehemence,
then,
her left hand
wants more darkness

YOU CAN'T FIND GOD OUTSIDE

FUNMINIYI AKINRINADE

This morn, you stretch like the wings of a bird,
You move closer to the window behind your bed,
Your eyes are fixated at the bedspread of heaven,
You begin to call your God in the distant skies,
In a skabash* tongue you don't understand.
You glide your fingers through your string of prayer beads,
So you don't lose track of your prayer points:
Lord, heal this land, this country won't end me
Your sweats, dripping like drops of blood
Your prayers, disturbed by drums of conundrum
You mutter words like, God why? God who?
God how? God where? God when? God what?
Why is wazobia a zoo of wobia?*
Who christened here a country?
How did we get deep in this mess?
Where are we heading to?
When will the messiah come?
What is the way out of this shithole?
Dear you,
You can't find God outside:
Not in the mi(d)st of your conundrum,
Not in the fist of words, feast of wars,
You can't find God outside;
When your men don't allow Him inside.

*Scabash means an unknown language
*wobia means rapacity/greedy individuals

25

SUMMER SOLSTICE

CARSON WOLFE

Stonehenge was dragged 200 miles
into astronomical alignment.
A massive effort, since it was built
5000 years ago, with no tools sharper
than the grief in my throat.

Spirituality is considered the reason
for assemblage, but no one knows the truth.
My guess is it was built to backdrop
England's most hedonistic
solstice party.

I dragged myself 200 miles
to this mystical land,
but all I bring is psychedelic Alice
and my rock
bottom.

A therapist might tell me why,
if I could stop drinking my paycheck.
I chug a bottle of red on entry,
liver cirrhosis,
my own ancient heritage.

Inside the stone circle,
druids worship the sun,
banging drums that crack
like vertebrae plagued
with Osteoporosis.

AT STONEHENGE

Alice and I synchronise our tongues
with little square invitations
to the longest day of the year.
I hug the healing stones,
everything is ok? Except,

my Nanna is dead.
I don't want a bad trip.
I spit out the tab of acid,
        maybe it's not too late?

        I don't want a bad trip.
            The stones pulsate like white blood cells, transfusing the red sunset.
            Maybe it's not too late.
         Alice is arrested. Her backpack contains a five year prison sentence.

           The stones pulsate like white blood cells, transfusing the red sunset.
      Police officer: *why is she carrying two ounces of weed?* My pupils eclipse.
Alice is arrested. Her backpack contains a five year prison sentence.
      Only twelve more hours of this.

      Police officer: *why is she carrying two ounces of weed?* My pupils eclipse.
         The moon is a jaundice kaleidoscope.
           Only twelve more hours of this.
              I think I was too late.

                I spat out the tab of acid,
                  but the moon is a jaundice kaleidoscope.
      I think I was too late.
My Nanna is dead.

A LIBRARY OF LIMBS

LEIGH CHADWICK

The Second Amendment says I am the Second Amendment. The pastor says thoughts and prayers. The wind says I am tired of carrying the smell of death. Some senators say too soon, too soon. Some senators say now is never the time. Some senators say now is the only time. The Second Amendment says everyone should buy a gun out of the trunk of a car in a Starbucks parking lot. The gun show says we're having a BOGO sale on body bags. The wind says I am also tired of carrying the sound of death. Mississippi says put a gun in your waistband when you go to Kroger to buy a gallon of skim and a package of Pampers. Tennessee says let's be more like Mississippi. California says puff, puff, pass. Texas says at least we're not Florida. Colorado says well, fuck. Colorado says did you not see the library of limbs. Colorado says sorry about the spilt blood in the produce aisle. Colorado says the popcorn is on us. The ghosts say there is no more room in the haunting place. The wind says still, it's the smell that's the worst. The south says if only. The Second Amendment says I will always be the Second Amendment. All senators say thoughts and prayers. Thoughts and prayers say sorry we are so useless. Jesus says if I had a gun that fucking cross wouldn't have had a chance.

TO SAY THE WORD LEMON IS TO SAY I WON'T ARGUE WITH YOU

Linda Blaskey

That is to say I have lived long and learned
when to pucker my mouth shut.
Old aunts and their bridge partners no longer want
to pinch the apples of my cheeks (which, of course,
is a way to say they are all dead.)

It is winter. I pull my sweater tighter,
double the socks on my feet. Do you care
the seat of my pants now sags?

We are bound to each other by years
of milk-meats eaten standing at the kitchen counter,
by the string of evenings with a shared shence of vodka & rocks
& twist of lemon.
(which is to say I don't speak when I drink—)

We pat each other in passing, air-kiss at bedtime,
a yank on the blankets and punch to the pillow
then, ah, sweet sleep while the moon's lemon-light
fingers its silent way about the room.

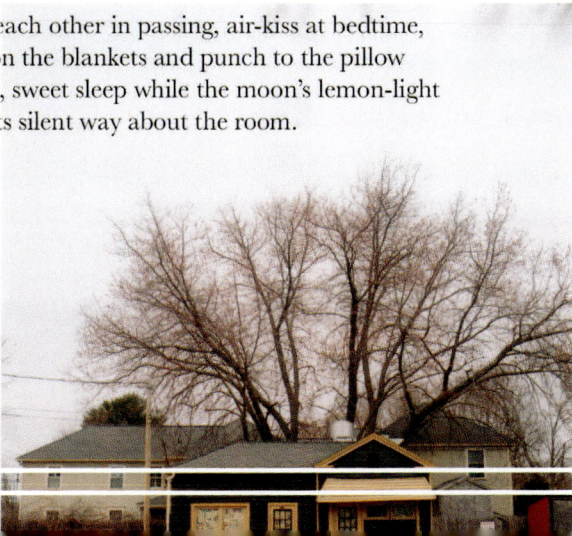

dignity of the [Swiss] creature

Gabrielle Jennings

dogs	must have sufficient daily contact with humans and, if possible, other dogs
	when kept in boxes or kennels for more than three months, dogs must have visual, auditory and olfactory contact with a fellow detainee in an adjoining enclosure
	requirement need not be fulfilled if dogs have contact with humans or other dogs outside their enclosure during the day for a total period of at least five hours
	mother and nurse bitches must be able to withdraw to the shelter of their puppies
	owners must take dog care classes
	barking inhibitors are illegal
cats	when kept individually must have daily contact with humans or eye contact with other cats
	can only be held alone in a cage of at least 10 sq. ft. for a maximum of three weeks
ferrets	sociable animals cannot be kept alone and need contact with their species
	should evolve in a group of at least two individuals
	humans or other animals cannot substitute
horses	
ponies	
donkeys	
mules	used to living in herds and must have visual, auditory and olfactory contact with another equine after weaning and up to the age of 30 months or until the start of their regular use
	young animals should be kept in groups
rabbits	sociable species should have appropriate social contact with fellow creatures
	should have at least olfactory and acoustic contact with others of the same species
	"social" windows such as a wire mesh placed on the walls of cages recommended but not required
	individual detention of young rabbits is not permitted during the first eight weeks of life

See Footnote Pg.56

gerbils	
guinea pigs	
rats	sociable animals must be kept in groups of at least two if one dies, it is suggested that another be temporarily rented
hamsters	Golden must be kept individually Dzougarie dwarf or Chinese can live in families
quails	sociable species of animals must be kept in groups of at least two specimens
pigeons	animals of sociable species are not allowed to be kept without having appropriate social contact with fellow creatures
canaries	
parakeets	sociable species, should not be kept alone
parrots	are sociable birds, should be kept at least in pairs or be given the opportunity to socialize regularly
goldfish	should never be detained alone but always in groups
turtles	reptiles are not social animals they mainly gather in large groups during the breeding season or around a big feast they can therefore be easily detained alone
hedgehog	is a wild animal, not a pet in Switzerland they live most of the time in urbanized areas, sick or injured animals are therefore often visible, and can be cared for temporarily by competent people
lobsters	can't be boiled alive
cows	bells are illegal

HOW TO DISSOCIATE

KEISHA CASSEL

Throw fried rice into a skillet, add oil.

Flex your feet: feel the pain radiate up your calf,
back down to the source.

Maybe, you'll flinch almost tripping over yourself.

Allow the sizzle of the rice to lure you into a trance.
And then, leave.
Walk out of your body-
                        through the laundry room-
                                        past your futon-
                                                out the door.

Walk until you're back in your grandmother's home.

Watch your sister run up and down the stairs
holding baskets of laundry.
Grandmother sits at the table reading over the mail.

Small you   -   baby you
stands on a stool overlooking the stove;
wearing your favorite skirt and a turtleneck stained with chocolate milk.

You're making gravy.
First, you, add oil and flour,

& *stir*

Until the flour & oil combo is on the verge of burning.
Next, add broth

& stir

& stir

The rice is starting to burn, it is time to leave.
Walk back to your body-
                        in the door-
                                past your futon-
                                        through the laundry room-

back to yourself.

When Will Our Memories Return From War

Keisha Cassel

I

My aunties use to say that Sunny's body
was all he got for fighting in that war.

The same Sunny who used to protect them
as they ripped and ran through the street

came back hollow.

"Sunny's eyes don't even shine no more
when he looks at his momma. All he can see

is blood, the men the government
named his enemy."

My aunties say Sunny still
write letters home they say,

I miss the way the soil pushes into my nails
when we prepare your garden for spring.

II

All of the people who placed war
on my grandmother's body seem to be doing well

and she is placing her fingers on
photos she framed and saying,

Now tell me your name again.

III

After the war, there is the moment
when tides subside.

Waves slowly retreating
from the shoreline

soft surfaces fading away
even the hard erode with time.

Running Late

for P.B.

Ty Holter

A friend who is older
who I met many years after

in another part of the country
who could only be in this south
a dream anachronism

is Mitchum in the dormer
while I dress the cul de sac
below in old clothes.

This is where I tore the corduroy
I say. And he seems to understand

pouring flannel
                    still on hangers
           all at once on the gardenias

saying this is only weather now
that we have somewhere to be.

OLD SPORT

{CLEM} {FLOWERS}

A forgotten name with the seeming occupation of:
"Football Player"

Scrawled beneath in an oddly beautiful, looping hand- the instant I read this specific inscription, I knew I had to buy this tawdry, paperback copy of *The Great Gatsby*. A quick flip thru, spying a load of pencil inscriptions & annotations, only sealed the deal.

I've already read it so many times in my life that I sometimes dream of the green lights just out of my reach, and hiding out while classy ragers I concocted go on as Max Roach swings until the sunlight crashes out over the breakers, but this was a guaranteed bit of magic.

A small door into another psyche, abandoned a dog's age ago, and at a rock bottom price, no less.

"Wanted to say goodbye to Jay G," over a particular patch of heartache towards the end--

"Gatsby *does* have ethics, " next to a recalled conversation--

"KICKBACK CORRUPTION {GATSBY}," scoring a passage of Gatsby displaying his silver tongue—

When I finish, I feel a bit low, similar to the first time I read this for the first time in high school.

This time, though, it isn't for Jay, Nick, or even the weird owl guy from the library ; it's for this kid, who clearly had a brilliant, insightful mind, but judging from the cover art & copyright date, I stand firm on the thought that, most likely, his was not a family that welcomed the life of the mind.

Makes me think of the kids I knew in high school, who were so smart, but their family only cared about the things "real men" do, and being beaten down on a muddy football field beats swing shift factory life any day.

I set this old book down in my lap & wonder where that kid, sharp as a copperhead fang, went in life.

Maybe mining.
Maybe oil.
Maybe dying in a war.

I put the book on the steeplechase bookcase in my apartment that my wife has had since middle school, and start to make dinner, while picturing the kid who had all this intelligence, got to go to college after all and ended up on a nice suburb, with a wife, kids, and a nice desk job.

 I smile as I watch the onions start to sizzle in the center of the pan.
"So we beat on, boats against the current, borne back ceaselessly into the past."

CLEAVE

VINCENT JAMES PERRONE

Prayer beads dangle in the all-too-know world—
that is, a collection of uninhabitable planets

becoming a single blade of light in the sky.
            Become a body cleaved. Play possum.

Play lorem ipsum. Become a body
redacted. A wolf licking a blade. You are employed
and you are the work of dying.

Forage in the food desert. Reaffirm
your position in the market. Sublimate
your flesh into a small business. Get something.

Sometimes husk—always

            the hum of the earth and the trauma
of blunt force. Sometimes the kill is clean,

blood settled, really just fallen trees.
Life becomes a series of suicides: possession,

repossession, dismemberment. What could be worse
than death without context? Which is to say,

derive any meaning you want from a body—
            a figure in ether, a cleaving of sign, us all

untethered like planets without gravity or the
            splay of light through a closed curtain.

Bromeliad

Navila Nahid

I am my Bromeliad,
        withering.
              I never needed your light.
I have my own
        tucked in shadow.
I hoard it
          for real darkness,
      the kind
un-vanquished in sun.

Yet I am still my Bromeliad,
        drooping
          within
             the warmth of you.

For you
      are *not* my light,
you can never feed me,
        grow me,
        love me.
You can't even find me on a map.
          I checked.
     You pointed at Antarctica.
I remind you
     I am warm-blooded.
        You call me a liar.

I tell you I can't lie
        when God is in everything
     and everything is me.
I can't lie
when I see him
and he sees—
    sin

Oh!
how I've sinned.
        Please God,
             forgive.

Forgive the un-truths
      I still spill
            to believe.
Forgive the prayers
      I let die.

Because I still talk to them,
           the little deaths.
I attend their funerals
        and spread their ashes
           back up
      to the cold, cold stars.

Some birth again,
          bloody—
       excavating me,
anew,
         as un-withered
           bloom
            of my Bromeliad.

SUMMER STORMS

DREW WAGNER

Street corner kids sell snow cones for quarters
no one buying, so the kids are thriving
eating simple syrup slosh from paper cones
losing profit; gaining prospect

the sky is split,
a crack in the clouds reveals electric bands
plasma snakes its way across the horizon, horizontal
the rain never comes to pull the hot lightning to Earth

Street corner kids sit, stand,
watch the fleeting energy light the sky
eating snow cones in eternal summer.

THE RIVER LINE STOP ON EAST BROAD STREET

MORGAN RIDGWAY

There's a minute before the train reaches the station I think—*don't move, stay put in this seat*, I've made a mistake. I've made a mistake but I'm somehow above my feet. I think about crying there on the platform, which is, by all accounts, appropriate. Like onions and garlic on a warming pan. I don't really know how to cook but I pretend just fine. The road saunters off and I trail behind looking for landmarks from before I grew into my clothes. Once I wore a suit jacket for eight years and it only looked right in 2006. I forgot how much I enjoyed the autumn here. The silence is charming and everything wants to be closer to the ground. Sometimes I think that I am neurotic for wanting things so profusely. Like my life depended on it. Truthfully, I want nothing more than I want myself. Mine is a self in succession and one day I'll be born again in the same place because even if no one remembers us, I will. I don't believe in individualism, which is a kind of American imagination. It's powerful to believe that you are connected to something even when the only body you have is your own. Like your incisors or your pinky finger. Like being on a dance floor and for a second forgetting the sound of loneliness. It is a fantasy, to disappear, but I thought it was a way of loving the world. Fantasy is much like desire and I have plenty of those. Whenever I'm anywhere but Palmyra I want to be in Palmyra because the sound of the pier reminds me of memories I've never had. I've always wanted the fiction of us most. It's half past three and a man is sitting on a bench studying his wrist. Wherever he is going it is someplace other than here. There's a single-story home at the end of the block. I never lived there except for in the summers and I am reminded of this feeling from when I was young and decidedly hopeful. My cousin opens the door with a cigarette loose in her mouth. "Look at you" she says and I smile like my mother. She pours hot water over a teaspoon of Folgers and we talk about time. For however long I forget about everything but our living and for a moment we are merely beautiful.

Thistles & Haggis

Yvonne Campbell

She visits her father's grave on Easter Sunday

I birthed three daughters and don't give a damn.

I think they're all rotten except for yeah, maybe the
youngest if I had to choose.

I came from the Highlands, known for thistles and haggis
and pipes wailing. That was then.

I have a few choice words for you.

You killed my mother,
and now you want me,
little sparkling Orphan Annie,
to be a star swimming in the ocean
with the other little fishes,
coming up to the surface.
No such chance.

Your gravesite is bare
except for the rocks.
Rocks and small pebbles
in a jar in the garage.

You passed, leaving
a suitcase of empty bottles
for a legacy, brown warm scotch.
It stung going down, twirled
around my mouth. I spewed,
could not take it, it burned.

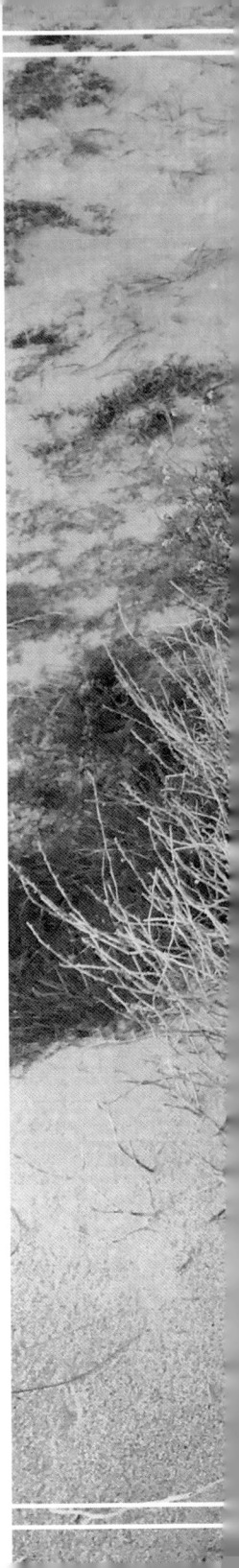

Dates waited outside,
afraid of the face
I couldn't look at.
My outfits, your leer.

It took out my guts
and replastered them around town.
Billboards, handbills, dances
at the Avalon Ballroom, the Fillmore.
The brown stain of come
on linens not washed . . .
The band music shaking me
by my fibers, my knots, my broken bones.

Too many trips down the Victorian flats
to forgotten dates.

I only wanted to be American.
In 1950 I married Don Campbell
and became Betty Crocker.
I can cook like her, I can make a man happy.
Take the chickies, put them in a flour sack.
Beat 'em to a pulp.

I birthed three daughters and don't give a damn.

I think they're all rotten except for yeah, maybe the
youngest if I had to choose.

I came from the Highlands, known for thistles and
haggis and pipes wailing. That was then.

INTRO

BLESSING OMEIZA OJO

At a gathering, I was called upon
to tell the world present and soon to die
who I am or who I would have become
if our ancestry doesn't determine our genetics.
'Long ago,' I say, 'something dark and durable
fell from the body of an iroko, somewhere in West Africa.
*abi, make I wash maself before man dem wash me.
There's a pool of laughter of what would have meant a slap
on my colour, on my identity. And I understood this
to be the only way to live anywhere without war,
I mean the shedding of blood for a brother shot somewhere
because he is not water– he doesn't flow well,
because he is dark– he blends with the night,
because his tongue is a stone– stone is a metaphor for us,
those learning to speak in a foreign tongue, yet not foreign,
those with alluring names which 'black' must prefix.
If I can't bear what you answer as a name,
do not call me names bounded by different genetic codes.
permit me to be nature, the beauty of existence.
Permit me to be black, the colour of resilience.

* Pidgin English

42

#2

god bless the gossip
of teenage girls with their mouths full of prophecy
curling bubble gum fingers knowing they're going nowhere

#1

eye contact red as
security cameras
with ticket stub tongue
knows just how to make a home feel like a two-star hotel

#3

truck bed breath, deadlift body through a blue morning my own personal un-televised
revival
survived by lonely people

Zoe Grace Marquedant

CRAYOLA WINDOWS

ANASTASIA
DIFONZO

It's the year 2001,
and I haven't seen my stepsister in months.
I'm the new girl in first grade

and it feels about the same.
Everyone keeps asking where my dad is.
I don't understand the truth,

so I tell them he died of a heart attack. Close enough.
The girl in the middle's named Margaret.
Her hair is blond, just like my stepsister's.

I wonder if she also has a brother,
and hope she won't think I'm a spoiled brat too.
It's my first Saturday here,

and 7am has come again.
I don't remember what it felt like last week,
only that I'm glad it's over. This was my first

full night's sleep in five years. I'm six.
The landscape here is still confusing.
Glasses and plates are intact, and my bedroom door

only opens when I open it. I feel a hole
in my chest, I think, only it's too heavy for that.
I'm missing a lot of light these days.

I suppose that's why yesterday,
Mom took me to the place where the man
asked me questions while I drew houses.

Perhaps he was meant to speak sun
into my crayola windows,
but the first time I gave him an answer,

he stared, speechless, for fifteen seconds.
I swallowed my words for the next fifteen years.
Later, I'd learn that he was a Forensic Psychologist,

tasked with flipping over the coins of my words
to unearth whatever dirt was hiding there.
I won't learn what he found.

Untitled

—after Michael Friedman

Benjamin
Niespodziany

It took hours. It had to be clear. The cloud passed overhead like some
kind of lie. Some kind of dying, fading stain. You called and you called
and forever we heard the ring but never did we find the booth, its
rumored hue, its dewdrop, its loss, its God.

PRAYERS & SINS

YUSUF BM

Death is handsome
Flowers are his appraisers
When bones slip silently
Beneath the mud-made bumpers
Hands stretch before God's face
"Oh widen this space"
And feet silently storm away.

THE PIXIES SELL OUT

MATT DETTMER

I learned so much about music from '02 through '04 I had a dorm room an internet connection
  headphones for when my roommates came back
My buddy sent me a downloaded copy of wilco with all the songs misnamed he's still never
  sure which one is which
One of those winters my brother was an hour away I had a car my parents left there while they
  were still overseas
I would pick it up from this garage downtown a big hulking thing I had to steer through streets
  crowded with snow crunch and salt onto 94 East
That stretch mostly runs south along the lake you can't see the water from the road

I'd pick my brother up on Sundays he was in a boarding school we'd leave campus and eat
  junk food in parking lots
I felt so old then driving on my own through some northern Chicago suburb we'd sit in theaters
  watching movies I saw Big Fish that way got quiet and cried at the end
The two of us driving around Illinois
On the way down or when I was with him or on the way back there'd be music
That car had a six disc changer this black box you'd pull out of the central console slide new
  ones in take old ones out
One of the CDs I'd bring down was the Pixies' second album

That was a big year for them they had these "Pixies sell out" t-shirts at their shows and
  later that fall I'd go see them
Hearing Kim Deal hold that oooh-ooooh out at the end of the set when they cut the lights and
  her voice was the only thing you could hear see taste or feel is a piece of time I keep in
  my pocket for whenever I need it
That was a big year for them they made a documentary with a thom yorke interview the
  reunion tour all of that
But that was also the year Kerry lost the year my parents came back and we started looking
  for a home
The year I'd drive south from Milwaukee on a highway over sheets of snow to see my
  brother shrieking along the way about aliens and monkeys bound for salvation

backroads

morgan ridgway

Come here,
let me wrap my arms
around you, there, sitting
on the hood of your broken-in truck

because for a moment it's just us
and wouldn't that be beautiful.
Your blue suede smooth laying,
waiting, my body velvet
on your back.

Take my cavernous being,
our star-faced memory,
take my wanting too.
Come here, my Brando boy,
taste September on my skin & swallow.

New Roses, Old Robots

rachel elizabeth

"The woman I aspire to be is already who I am"
I said that five times in the mirror today then walked outside
And got stung by a wasp

I'm living with a girl who's hair is longer than mine and patience thinner
than her goal weight
She has a stern voice and a child's face
The perfect foil to all my flaws

L.A makes me wish I didn't fear men as much as I do
So I could be getting railed at noon
By some director I met on Hinge who takes everything but his hat off

After washing him off my face, I'd condescendingly ask
"why does every man in film dress like a retired baseball player?"
And he would laugh loud
Knowing that if he makes me feel clever
I'll leave without him having to ask me to.

LA BREA

VINCENT JAMES PERRONE

At the La Brea Tar Pits you vision yourself preserved.
I imagine an archive of debris. Oil soaked hair, splinters
of bone. Both of us fetal—suspended in black amber.
Our breath slow bubbles to the surface. Preservation

is the goal but bread goes stale—one relic is holy
as the next. And all the pitch in Hancock Park becomes
a monastery for unabsolved tourists. Ground sloths
and dire wolves and missing links are all indifferent

to our presence. We're transfixed as if expecting
the tar to part like the heavy doors of a church. It seems
like the very science of belief has brought us here
today. To purchase keepsake keychains that will survive us.

That's when we think about death as another kind of body
like a black lake full of things others told us about.
That's when we realize we're unprepared for excavation—
so we go into LACMA and buy more keychains.

MY BEST FRIEND THE BEAR

GABRIELLE JENNINGS

In 2019, Casey,
a three year old North Carolina boy was found deep in the forest
behind his grandmother's house.
He was crying and tangled in thorn bushes.

My best friend the bear
kept me safe.

In 1955, Ida Mae, a two year old,
went missing in Montana.
She was found after two days of pouring rain.

I was cuddled
and
comforted by a bear.

In 1888, a two year old girl
was found two miles away from home,
in a deep valley.

I slept by a bear that kept me warm at night.

In 1869, Katie, a three year old from Michigan
went missing overnight.

A big doggie stayed with me.

*See Footnote Pg.56

POETRY
CONTRIBUTORS

Kevin Bertolero (he/him): is the founding editor of Ghost City Press and is the author of three collections of poetry, most recently Love Poems (Bottlecap Press, 2020). His non-fiction book on gay cinema is forthcoming in 2021 with Another New Calligraphy. He is currently studying in the MFA program at New England College. You can follow him on Twitter @KevinBertolero.

Ben Kline (he/him): lives in Cincinnati, Ohio. His chapbook SAGITTARIUS A* landed in October 2020 from Sibling Rivalry Press. His chapbook DEAD UNCLES rises from Driftwood Press in May 2021. A poetry reader for The Adroit Journal, his work is forthcoming or can be found in THRUSH, The Holy Male, The Indianapolis Review, Limp Wrist, DIAGRAM, Hobart, A&U Magazine, and many other publications. You can read more at https://benklineonline.wordpress.com/. Twitter: BenKlinePoet

Jen Gupta (she/her): is a middle school English teacher, writer, avid hiker, and horse lover. She lives in Somerville, Massachusetts with her husband and their seven house-plants.

Linda Blaskey (she/her): is the recipient of two Fellowship Grants in Literature from Delaware Division of the Arts. She is poetry editor emerita forBroadkill Review; coordinator for Dogfish Head Poetry Prize, and editor at Quartet,an online poetry journal. Her work has been included in Best New Poets, and the North Carolina Poetry on the Bus project. She is author of Farm; of White Horses; and co-author of Walking the Sunken Boards.

Carson Wolfe (they/them): during lockdown, Carson adopted a cat to live like an eccentric writer, but now spends most of their time salvaging the poems her keyboard paws delete - rather than actually writing them. Surviving work can be found in Stone of Madness Press, Kissing Dynamite, and Brag Magazine amongst others. www.carsonwolfe.com Twtitter: @vincentvanbutch

Yusuf BM (he/him): is a writer, poet, graphic designer, passionate photographer, motivational speaker and prolific blogger. He is the 3rd winner of Korean Nigeria Poetry Competition (2017-Student Category) He is currently the Administrative secretary of Hill – Top Creative Arts foundation, member of the SEVHAGE Publishers, Raising New Voices, Nigerian Writers Forum, as well as the CEO of Mammoth Spectrum Media and Yusuf BM Sickle Cell Foundation. Facebook: Yusuf BM Instagram: @Official_Yusufbm Twitter: @Official_YBM1

Sodiq Oyekanmi: is a poet, playwright and thespian; a student of the University of Ibadan, where he currently studies Theatre Arts. He co-judged the AKUKO inaugural literary competition [poetry category] with Rosed Serrano. His works have appeared / forthcoming in Pigeonholes, The Shallow Tales Review, African Writer Magazine, Brittle Paper, Black Youth Magazine, The Drinking Gourd, Rigorous Magazine, Kalahari Review, Praxis Magazine and trampset. A hopeless romantic who tweets @sodiqoyekan.

Yvonne Campbell (she/her): named after Hollywood starlet, Yvonne DeCarlo, by my father because he liked her legs. Raised by sheet metal worker father and Scottish immigrant mother who harbored fantasies of a stage career but settled for being the life of the party. A child writer, I published my own newspaper, and submitted to the Oakland Tribune's children's page. I've written during stints as an ESL teacher, stock broker, waitress, barista, and union organizer. Re-locating to Oregon, I write memoir flash fiction and poems. Currently I'm completing a dystopic novel, HandyFam about the price of living in the Tech infused San Francisco environs.

Whitney Hansen (she/they): is a poet and fiction writer living in Texas. She has been published in Poetry Superhighway and other fine journals on the web.

Drew Wagner (they/them): A sentient game of "exquisite corpse." Twitter: @TinCan_Wagner

Yuu Ikeda (she/her): is a Japan based poet. She loves writing, reading mystery novels, and drinking sugary coffee. She writes poetry on her website. https://poetryandcoffeedays.wordpress.com/ Her published poems are "On the Bed" in <Nymphs>, "Seeds" in <Tealight Press>, "Dawn" in <Poetry and Covid>, and more. Her Twitter and Instagram: @yuunnnn77

Matt Dettmer (he/him): a writer, musician, and physician currently practicing in Cleveland, OH. His work has previously been published in Talk Vomit, The Harpy Hybrid Review, and The Gravity of the Thing. Instagram: @mrdettmer

Clem Flowers (they/them): A queer, soft spoken southern transplant living in the colossal shadow of a mountain range in Utah. They enjoy cooking, watching old films, and making many trips to a local bird sanctuary. They live in a cozy apartment with their wonderful wife & sweet calico kitty Luna.

Navila Nahid (she/her): is a writer and published poet, currently residing in Brooklyn, NY. Her need for writing began young when putting pen to paper seemed more natural than going outside. Now, she creates to pull solace from the world. Her published works can be found in Sky Island Journal, Cephalopress, Free Verse Revolution Literary Magazine and Beyond Words Literary Magazine. She can also be found on Instagram as @seasalt.rose My website is: slnmten.wordpress.com

Morgan Ridgway (they/them): is a dancer, historian, and Gemini from Philadelphia, PA. They are currently completing a PhD in history thinking about gathering, care, and joy. Their work has appeared in CP Quarterly, Horse Egg Literary, Indigo Literary Journal, among others. Twitter: @morgan_ridgway

Akinrinade Funminiyi Isaac (he/him): fondly called Esv_Keks is a Nigerian realtor and writer with works appearing in Writers Space Africa Magazine, Olney Magazine, Praxis Magazine, Word Rhymes and Rhythm (WRR) Anthology, Scion Magazine and elsewhere. He's an Associate Editor at PoeticAfrica and the initiator of two poetry collections: Si(gh)lent Night, a night of sighs and wanders (2017) and 60 Seconds Silence (2020). Facebook: https://www.facebook.com/akinrinadeoluwafunminiyi Twitter: https://twitter.com/esv_keks?s=09 Instagram: https://www.instagram.com/invites/contact/?i=1phuvsuhlx5u&utm_content=ypr75d LinkedIn: https://www.linkedin.com/in/funminiyi-akinrinade

Blessing Omeiza Ojo (he/him): is a Nigerian poet and teacher. His works have been published or forthcoming in Split Lip Magazine, Roughcut Press, Lunaris Review, Last Girls Club, Artmosterrific, Trampoline and elsewhere. His poem, "Everything Around Us Sings" was selected for publication at the Castello di Duino 2021 International Poetry and Theatre Competition. In 2020, Omeiza was named the Arts Lounge's Literature Teacher of the Year. He was a shortlist of Eriata Oribhabor Poetry Prize 2020, semi-finalist for Jack Grapes Poetry Prize 2020, and the winner, 9th Korea-Nigeria Poetry Prize (Ambassador Special Prize). He is currently a creative writing instructor at Jewel Model Secondary School, Abuja, where he has coached winners of national and international writing prizes.

Ben Niespodziany (he/him): is a Pushcart Prize nominee and Best Microfiction nominee. His work has appeared in Wigleaf, Hobart, Maudlin House, Fence, and various others. A returned Peace Corps volunteer, he now works nights in a library in Chicago. **socials / website: neonpajamas / neonpajamas.com**

Andrew Hahn (he/him): received his MFA from Vermont College of Fine Arts and is the author of the poetry chapbook God's Boy (Sibling Rivalry Press, 2019). His work is featured in or forthcoming from Barren Magazine, Aquifer: The Florida Review Online, Lunch, Pithead Chapel, Crab Creek Review, Crab Fat Magazine, Glass: A Journal of Poetry, and Rappahannock Review among others. He is a Best of the Net nominee and was listed in Yes, Poetry's Best and Faves of 2019.

Okoli Stephen Nonso: is a Nigerian writer whose poems have previously appeared in Feral Journal, Ebedi Review, Ngiga Review, Praxis Magazine, African writer, Adelaide Literary Magazine New York, Tuck magazine, and elsewhere. His short story has appeared in Best of African literary magazine. He has contributed in both national and international pages and anthologies. A joint winner of the May 2020 Poets in Nigeria (PIN) 10 day poetry challenge, first runner-up in the fresh voice foundation Poetry contest, and a third prize winner of the Akuko magazine inaugural prize for Poetry 2021. His bio was included in the 'Who's Who of Emerging Writers 2021' by Sweetycat press publication. Twitter @OkoliStephen7

Vincent James Perrone (he/him): is the author of the full-length poetry book, "Starving Romantic" (11:11 Press, 2018), the forthcoming chapbook, "Travelogue for the Dispossessed" (Ghost City Press, 2021), and a contributor to "Collective Voices in the Expanding Field" (11:11 Press, 2020). Recent work published and forthcoming from The Indianapolis Review, Emerge Literary Journal, Levee Magazine, and more. Say hi on twitter @spookyghostclub or at vincentjamesperrone.com

Shannong Frost Greenstein (she/her): resides in Philadelphia with her children, soulmate, and persnickety cats. She is the author of "Pray for Us Sinners," a collection of fiction from Alien Buddha Press, and "More.", a poetry collection by Wild Pressed Books. Shannon is a former Ph.D. candidate in Continental Philosophy and a multi-time Pushcart Prize and Best of the Net nominee. Her work has appeared in McSweeney's Internet Tendency, Pithead Chapel, Bending Genres, Epoch Press, X-R-A-Y Lit Mag, and elsewhere. Follow her at shannonfrostgreenstein.com or on Twitter @ShannonFrostGre.

Keisha Cassel: is a multidisciplinary artist currently based in State College, PA They recently received their MA in Creative Writing from Royal Holloway, University of London and have a BA in Music from Smith College. Keisha is a 2019 Fulbright Semifinalist and a 2020 Pushcart prize nominee. You can find their work in Variety Pack, Call and Response journal(forthcoming) and their micro-chap Constructs(Ghost City Press).

Luke Larkin (he/him): is a San Diego based poet with a cat named Klaus. Her work can be found or is forthcoming in Anti-Heroin Chic, Gnashing Teeth Publishing, Sledgehammer Lit, Punk Noir Magazine, Kalopsia Literary Journal, Salt & Citrus, and Drunk Monkeys. She is on Instagram @anastasia.difonzo and Twitter @anmidaludi. Linktree: linktr.ee/anastasia.difonzo

Zoey Grace Marguedant (she/her/hers): is a queer writer. She earned her B.A. from Sarah Lawrence College and her M.F.A. from Columbia University. Her work has been featured in the Cool Rock Repository, Analog Cookbook, Schuylkill Valley Journal, and Talk Vomit. Follow @zoenoumlaut

Dale Cottingham: I am of mixed race, part Choctaw, part White. I am a Breadloafer, won the 2019 New Millennium Award for Poem of the Year and am a finalist in the 2021 Great Midwest Poetry Contest. I live in Edmond, Oklahoma.

Ty Holter (he/him): is a writer and welder in Denver. His work has appeared in Protean and 3 Moon Magazines. Find him on Twitter @tylerleeholter.

Leigh Chadwick (She/her): is the author of the chapbook, Daughters of the State (Bottlecap Press, 2021), and the poetry coloring book, This Is How We Learn How to Pray (ELJ Editions, 2021). Wound Channels, her full-length poetry collection, and Pretend I Am Real, a novel written in vignettes, will be simultaneously released by ELJ Editions in February of 2022. Her writing has appeared or is forthcoming in Salamander, Heavy Feather Review, Indianapolis Review, and Milk Candy Review, among others. Find her on Twitter at @LeighChadwick5.

Gabrielle Jennings (She/her): is a multimedia writer and artist whose work mines our collective unconscious by using appropriation in conjunction with the autobiographical. Her poetry has appeared in Fence, and Terror House. She teaches in the Graduate Art program at ArtCenter College of Design, and lives with her family and menagerie in Los Angeles.

FOOTNOTES: "Dignity of the (swiss) creature" P. 30-31: Swiss Federal Food Safety and Veterinary Affairs *https://www.blv.admin.ch/blv/fr/home/tiere/tierschutz/heim-und-wildtier-haltung.html*

"My Best Friend The Bear" P. 51: Bear-3-year-old boy lost in freezing forest for two days says bear kept him safe *https://www.yahoo.com/entertainment/3-year-old-boy-lost-freezing-forest-two-days-says-bear-kept-safe-101510537.html*

Tales of an Educated Debutante, Casey and the Bear *https://m.facebook.com/talesofaneducateddebutante/photos/a.1672324146342981/2229407743967949/?type=3&theater*

PHOTOGRAPHY

Edward Lee: their poetry, short stories, non-fiction and photography have been published in magazines in Ireland, England and America, including The Stinging Fly, Skylight 47, Acumen and Smiths Knoll. He is currently working on two photography collections: 'Lying Down With The Dead' and 'There Is A Beauty In Broken Things'. He also makes musical noise under the names Ayahuasca Collective, Orson Carroll, Lego Figures Fighting and Pale Blond Boy. His blog/website can be found at https://edwardmlee.wordpress.com

Halle Preneta (she/her): enjoys writing short romance, sci-fi, and horror stories along with poetry and gets her ideas from random life experiences and fanfiction. When she's not writing, she's either watching YouTube or playing Animal Crossing. Her Twitter handle is @YaTheatreNerd and you can check out more of her work here: https://sites.google.com/view/halle-preneta/home

Jeson Melvin (he/him): is a father, husband, grandfather, high school soccer coach, and metals processing center supervisor, who lives just outside of Pittsburgh. His wife accuses him of having more pictures of "stupid shit" on his phone than of his family. She's not wrong. His poems have recently appeared in Rat's Ass Review, Kitchen Sink Magazine, The Electric Rail, The Front Porch Review, Shambles, Spillover, Olney, Last Leaves, and Zero Readers, among others. Instagram: @jasonmelvin5 Twitter: @jason5melvin

Raye Hendrix (she/they): is a writer from Alabama. Her micro-chapbook, Fire Sermons, is forthcoming this Summer from Ghost City Press. Raye is the winner of the 2019 Keene Prize for Literature and Southern Indiana Review's 2018 Patricia Aakhus Award. Her work has been featured in Poetry Daily, 32 Poems, Shenandoah, Cimarron Review, Poetry Northwest, Zone 3, and elsewhere. She holds degrees from Auburn University and an MFA from the University of Texas at Austin, and is currently a PhD student at the University of Oregon studying Deafness, Disability, and Poetry. She teaches writing and is an officer in her union.

Denise Nichole Andrews (she/her): MFA, is the Editor in Chief of The Hellebore Press & Founder of HUES. She teaches and resides in Sacramento, CA with her partner of ten years. Her recent photography and writing can be found in Hooligan Mag & Parentheses Journal. She enjoys lavender lattes, thrifting for vintage finds, and being a friend to all. For tender tweets follow her on Twitter @DNicholeAndrews.

Thaina Joyce (she/her): is a Brazilian-American poet and educator based in Maryland. Her poetry has been featured at Sledgehammer Lit, Olney Magazine, Lumiere Review, and elsewhere. She hopes her work will empower, connect the human experience, and evoke new perspectives. Find her on IG: @thainawrites Twitter: @teedistrict Read more: https://linktr.ee/teedistrict

Syreeta Muir (she/her): writes and takes pictures of weird, sad stuff. You can find her writing in TL;DR Press's Women's Anthology: Carrying Fire, The Ampersand Project, The Passage Between, and The Horror Tree: Trembling With Fear. Her pictures are in Barren Magazine. If this is simply not enough, fear not, find her on Twitter as @hungryghostpoet, she will be more than happy to make you feel weird/ sad there, too.

Sol Macias (she/her): Two decades on planet Earth and counting. I love many things, but trees are at the top of the list. Instagram: solmaciasss https://www.are.na/sol-macias

Rebekah D. (she/her/they): Wife, mom, stepmom, daughter, sister, friend, military veteran, healthcare worker, pet mom, empath. Honeycreek Photography. The image of the stacked hands springs from my volunteer work with a local nursing home and hospice provider. As a loved one nears the end of their journey, the family is offered an opportunity for this type of photo, memorializing their hands together forever.

The bride with the butterfly on her bouquet was a truly meaningful encounter. While taking photos after the wedding, a butterfly spontaneously landed on her bouquet, and stayed for a surprisingly long time. This particular bride felt a spiritual connection to butterflies and believed that this was the spirit of her deceased grandmother visiting her and giving her blessing to the wedding. It was a deeply profound moment for the couple.